Woman, Woman

Angela de Hoyos

Arte Público Press
Houston
1985

ements

This publication is made possible through a grant from the National Endowment for the Arts and the Texas Commission on the Arts.

Some of these poems have appeared previously in:

The Pawn Review; Imagine International Poetry Journal; Hojas Poéticas; La Palabra; Maize; Caracol; Revista Chicano-Riqueña; Tejidos; Revista Río Bravo; Selected Poems; Chicanos: Antología histórica y literaria; Latin American Women Writers: Yesterday and Today; Woman of Her Word; Malintzin.

Arte Público Press
University of Houston
University Park
Houston, Texas 77004

Contents

Introduction by Rolando Hinojosa

"que me tangit,
vocem meam
audit"

"when you touch me,
you hear
my voice"

(Latin verse inscribed on a
Roman Country Estate Bell)

Reader Beware

The present writer finds it only fair to warn the reader lucky enough to find this book: beware!, you're in the hands of a poet. You're meant to read slowly, to ponder, and to reread before moving on to the next entry by Ms. de Hoyos. Your time, then, could not be better spent.

The work begins with **Woman, Woman** *the titular poem, and is then followed by the challenging—and haunting—* **Go Ahead, Ask Her**; *the pace doesn't slow down, either, it merely speeds up and dares and prods the reader to read on.*

The present writer did read on and considers himself fortunate, and challenged, too. There are some tough truths in there and some harsher realities, too. But here's something you won't find: mewling, puling, a hands-on-forehead begging for understanding.

The style? Understated, and since the words are clear enough, they need no deciphering; it is poetry as it is meant to be.

And, it's a very, very personal work. It speaks to me as a person, and it will speak to those who buy and keep the book.

One of my favorites, **Notice: To a Would-Be Quixote** *is included here as are* **Up to a Certain Point** *and the pointed* **A (Somewhat Gory)** *coup de grace.*

And then Ms. de Hoyos presents us with a bonus: that fine, crackling Spanish voice can be heard in Poemanónimo Número Equis *and the rollicking* Would You Please Rephrase the Question?, *among others.*

I find it of little value to talk on form and structure in this instance since the content carries the day here. Ms. de Hoyos does as she pleases—as she should—and it pleases very well indeed. Look at To Honor The Fact, *and you'll see what I mean. And it's a funny book, too; and it's meant to be, of course.*

Why don't you start with **How to Eat Crow on a Cold**

Sunday Morning *and* **Ancient History**? *And then, for a sustained piece, cut your teeth on* **In the House of Love**.

As said, we're in the hands of a poet, and one we can trust to startle and to surprise us. You see, only good can come after a life lived as a labor of love.

Woman, Woman

Woman, Woman

climb up
that ladder
bring down
the moon
or she
will tattle

tattle falsehood
to the skies
(and who
can tell
the truth
from lies?)

that it
is you
forever Eve
who rules
mere man
without
reprieve

Go Ahead, Ask Her

. . . . . . is it
not true
that when
a woman
cries
all the
gentlemen
console
her

but when
a wife
cries
she cries
alone?

Ten Dry Summers Ago

you could've planted Bermuda grass,
your neighbor to the right says.
But no, you didn't
   . . . and yes it's true
   your life
      never depended upon it . . .

so now I have to landscape
this bare and godless ground
that keeps eroding
   into flyaway dust
   changing hands
      as easily as identity

have to dance, pivoting
—as a Chicano would say—
      "en un daimito"
   watering this wasteland

have to keep it moist
until it grows
   until there's room enough
   to hold
      your god and mine

Up to a Certain Point

When I know my sky
to be blue
    and your brush insists
    on painting it
              purple

to fit the rage
of your colors

when I know my world
to be round
    round as the warm
    ring of love
        and you plane it
        into a square
precise and cold
and mathematical

:how differently
we re-act
    to the stimulus
    of life!
        because we arrive
        hand in hand
but always
at opposite conclusions.

People could almost say
that we complement
    each other.
    And I might add:

Opposites attract
but only
    up to a certain point.

    Your northpole
    has very little
    in common
    with my south . . .

Words Unspoken

you may boast that in your prison
you have locked me for no reason
save the fact that in your house
    there shouts a man

and I'll stay—NOT to add glory,
O my conqueror, to your story—
but because my instinct tells me
    that perhaps

underneath all that bravado
quakes a hopeless desperado
who longs to win a battle
    now and then

A (Somewhat Gory) *coup de grace*
or
"Pero Qué Clase de Chingaderas Son Estas?"*

I mistook the intentions
    of a red
    (poison)rose

and now my heart
    H A N G S
    in mid-air
                like a
                sacrificed lamb

dripping blood
    from my
    Achilles heel
                to my
                naked toes.

---

*roughly translated, "Are You Trying to Screw Me Up or
Something?"

Words Inspired by Wayward Husbands, Pontifical Lovers and Innocuous Deviants

the
distance
between
thee
and
me

. . . . therein
lies
the
poem

You Will Grow Old

forever comparing me
with your dream woman
—that goddess
    of fantasy
    of matchless perfection
        defying correction
    yet always
    so conspicuously absent—
while I go about
grinding my teeth
on the thankless endless
daily task:
        dusting your wings.

I too
will age . . .
        for obvious reasons.

"Ex" Marks the Spot

oh how you laughed
and laughed
and laughed
when you left me
d a n g l i n g
from a limb

but now
ha! ha!
the joke's on you
because I learned to
h a n g
and thereby
saved my skin

oh yes
my ghost
is real
and . . . your smile?
your smile
is grim

Lesson in Semantics

Men, she said,
  sometimes
    in order to
     say it

it is
  necessary
    to spit
     the word.

The Deadlier of the Species
or
"Not All Saints Are Women
Nor All Women, Saints"

who are you
and who am I

women
(sometimes beyond reason)

we murder man
our only son
in sanctimonious treason . . .

        tú quién eres
        y yo quién soy

        mujeres
        (a veces sin razón)

        matamos al hombre
        nuestro unigénito
        en santificada traición . . .

Portrait: Non-Progress

How can I hold you
    mold you fold you
into an artist's
dream of a demi-god
if you don't
        sit still?

If you're always chasing
some labyrinthian
    Mad-Corinthian
    project anonymous
    —and you the official
you the official
supplier of stars
to keep your
Way-Out world illumined?

    (So you squeeze our time
    till we haven't the space
        on earth
        to place
    one golden moment
    for us: like
            what are you
            doing tonight?)

How can I paint you?
I mean when I see you
see you
        bigger than canvas

and my desperate
mixed-up oils
are not the colors
　　—not the weightless
　　wondercolors—
of your super-orbit life?
And your profile
turns liquid
　　—I mean
　　just plain liquid
　　running away from me
　　from my
　　purple-passion palette—
and not a good cup
in the place
to scoop it up.
　　　　　　　It scares me.

Two Poems: Inebrieties

Poem To (What A) Wine/
Poema Al (Qué) Vino

into the passion-seas
  of your eyes
quite by mistake
    (adventure-bent)
    I have fallen

no one can save me:
  I must swim
    or sink

         Poema Al (Que) Vino

         ya no estoy sola:

            en el fondo de mi copa
            un rostro se asoma . . .

         . . . y yo que esperaba
         salvarle el pellejo
         a este poemamomento
         tan ebrio
            y tan mío

Fairy Tale/Cuento de Hadas

to Eduardo Díaz
to Beverly Sánchez Padilla

She was a bona-fide
storybook princess.
        Romantic.
        Impractical.
A delicate princess of innocence
born to blush
        in the midst of a cynical
        go-go buy-buy world.
        (O yes, María, who knows why, but
        anachronisms do happen.)

And so she dreamed and dreamed.
She dreamt of
        Prince charming and the
        happily-ever-after.
Fantasizing halcyon utopias
she convinced herself
        that all of God's creatures
        (for her sake)
were ideally endowed
with the best of
        Platonic aspirations,
        gently lulled
in the poetry of perfection.

Until one night (the story relates)
she discovered her consort-prince
        in the form of a macho-man
        stepping out on the sly.

Desperate
    she hit the panic-button
    shouting
        HELP!!! O MY GOD . . .
        DO SOMETHING!
But God just sat
    on His throne in the sky
    and never so much as
            blinked an eye

. . . and the story is vague
as to what happened then
but she never never never again
blindly believed
        in deities, or
           in men.

Poemanónimo Número Equis

Hombre casado . . .
    esa yegua sin rienda
    que viene perdida
    que te mira te mira
       te
       m m m m m m i r a , , , , ,
        no te pertenece.

    Déjala pasar.

Se Pasa Uno de Tonta

:cuando se sonríe a solas
:cuando contesta entredientes
con un gesto
de enfado
:cuando ya no se puede
discutir con él
sin que te levante
la voz
:cuando no llega en
toda la noche
. . . .
. . . .
. . . .
. . . . . .
. . . . .
. . .
.
repito:
se pasa uno de tonta

Good Politics: For Gushing Ladies

you may
kiss and
hug
    the men

you may
hug and
kiss
    the guys

but
NO-NO-NO
       the husbands

—you will
a l i e n a t e

        the wives

To Honor the Fact

THE TIME: going back in memory
    to fit
        the space required
    for this play
    in words   in deeds   in-wards

THE PLACE: a backyard of
a house—your house,
my house,
        anybody's house

THE SCENE: an old-fashioned
afternoon, perfect for
children growing up
beneath the silent
weight of predetermined
sexist roles

CHARACTERS: he and she
        (as playmates)

He says: let's play at being
    grand and great.
    Privileged male, naturally,
    I'm first.

—Privileged male? Since when?
—Since Adam, madam.
—I see. Okay. Privileged male,
you start first.

31

(at this point, he
means no harm
so there is no
cause for alarm)

—"To be or not to be . . ."
to shake or not
to shake the spear . . .
Sayyyyy!!! Methinks I
am GREAT. And GRAND
is my middle name!

So saying, he takes
the longest stick
and with it measures
all his qualities
—the pure
             the sterling
                          the gold
                          the alloys
             the varnished and the non—
then he proceeds
             (as self-appointed judge)
to hang the best
             the brightest
                          the greenest
laurels on his head,
                          until she
                          scowls and
stamps her foot
and moans:
             O Jeez, *nothing*
             will be left
                          for MEEEEEEE!

And then reluctant
he begins

with that same
long stick
to size her up . . .

                    and he runs
                         out
                         of
                            stick.

Respuesta de las Palabras, I

"hazlas, poeta,
haz que se traguen todas
sus palabras."

—Octavio Paz

Somos tus hijas, O noble bardo,
y cierto es
que bajo pluma y tinta
algunos hombres-machos
nos han prostituido.

Mas no por eso dejamos
de ser dignas,
pues en muchas ocasiones
tu propio "ego" se elevó
con nuestro aliento.

Ahora, si ya no quieres
que cantemos a tu gloria
—si prefieres hijas mudas,
sin palabras—

pues nos vamos al NuncaMás
O padre nuestro, distinguido,
poeta indiscutible, culto,
sí, pero malagradecido.

Reply of the Words, II

words are like mares
      (my dear amigOctavio)

:treat them
      g e n t l e
      —with a loose rein—
                  if you
                  want them
                  to behave

Virgin Mother

within my virgin hand
your kiss in bloom
came to nestle

in my bosom, your son
—my arms
of a madonna
upon my lap maternal
to sleep
I lulled you both

and whoever presumes to judge me
was not born
a child of God

Madre Virgen

entre mi mano virgen
se anidó el beso flor
de tu boca

entre mi seno, tu niño
—mis brazos
de madona

en mi regazo mater
los arrullé
a los dos

y el que pretenda juzgarme
no nació
hijo de Dios

Epistle to Mireya
:your poems

being
     —as you are—
a dual citizen
of life and death
         circumstance
cannot wholly claim you:

    in being and non-being
    you are always
        a step
        or two
        ahead of Time

I see you shuttle
back and forth
    —an expert
        vacillating—
compromising with dreams
or retreating
       when necessary
to the realm
of your mystic world
where nothing
      can wound you . . .

yet
    in each encounter
    you leave something
      you leave something
      of your self

an essence
   like this wistful rose
   that came to me
     —with its shy
        apologetic smile—
out of some
forbidden garden

and I agree
   "Springtime in New York
     —incredible with beauty!"

Where the Wound Lies

because I go
    like the professed
        sinner repentant
to the altar
of your baptismal flame
    I am saved

despite your
        sculptor-love
whose whimsy kneads
           and molds
           and fires
then breaks
the free-form
of my fasting body
        to make
        me whole
yet thankful
I accept
    these carnal gifts
    of you
        Eros
and wear them
as I would
flawless jewels

    (how can you
    know that I
    have bled

        the way
        and back
        biting the dust
        to wear
        your name?)

. . . the wound lies
                          not
in your infliction
        but in my
            expectations . . .

Notice: To a Would-Be Quixote

I am looking for a shoulder
   —must be spillproof!—
somewhat resilient
broad enough to cradle
my enormous fool's head . . .

   (I need to have
      a good hard cry
         for now
            and again)

Un Llanto en Seco

dos mares lindos
eran mis ojos
. . . pero se secaron
de lágrimas

    y ¿sabes por qué?

porque vino la vida
—cortesana embustera—
y tú tan naive que eres
te contó las muelas

   . . . dos mares
           lindos
           eran mis ojos . . .

Would You Please Rephrase the Question?

. . . lo que me molesta
es que me diriges
la pregunta
con aire autocrático
de esa manera tuya—Chaz!
al golpe del hacha
y ni siquiera
tuve tiempo
de armarme
para contestarte
debidamente

. . . oye chiquitito
que no has oído del Women's Lib?
hasta Alurista lo afirma:
ya las mujeres no te piden permiso
te dicen
"quiero hacer esto . . ."
y sanseacabó

así es que
hazme el favor
—por lo que te dé más coraje—
would you please rephrase the question?

On the Dangers Encountered
for the Sake of Society

There is infamy in the air
—a greed—
   a need
   to do evil.

One has but to venture forth
   (for the sake of society)
to the smorgasbord of life
and
   zzzooooommmmmm
      the daggers
      venom laden
whistle by
looking for likely targets.

With man stalking
his own kind
   —now, more than ever—
I don't dare abandon
   the comparable safety
     of my own cage . . .

How to Eat Crow
on a Cold Sunday Morning

you start on the wings
n i b b l i n g
                    apologetic-like
because after all
    it was you
    who held the gun
    and fired pointblank
    the minute you saw the
    whites of their eyes
just like the army sergeant
always instructed you.

—Damn it, this thing's
gonna make me sick!

—No it won't. Go on. Eat the
blasted thing
                (for practice)

because you'll be sicker
later on
            when your friends
            start giving you
an iceberg for a shoulder.

. . . So the giblets are dry
and tough.
            But you can
            digest them.

It's the gall bladder
—that green bag of biliousness—
   wants to gag your throat
   in righteous retribution

refuses to budge
won't go up or down, just
               sticks there

makes you wish that long ago
you'd learned how to eat
a pound of prudence
          instead.

O Reckless Atlas:

upon your broad shoulders
you alone
    carry the
    crystal heaven
    of my
    dream world

whoooooops . . . . . . i c u i d a d o !

        no se
        te vaya
        a caer

Virginia Gill, Visual Artist
Bakes a Cake
for the Arts Committee Meeting

dark chocolate
ribbons
swirling
       around fingerlicking
       y y y u m m m m y y y
       white meringue
can melt away
the strongest case
of human resistance

Virginia bakes
and bakes
in frank disguise:
          Banana Nut Bread
          German Coffee Cake
          Creme de Menthe Pie
          Pane Italiano

       Ageless delights, these!
       All made from scratch.

. . . and how logical
          the switch
:to exchange
ceramic kiln
for kitchen oven.
          To produce
edible works of art

love-crafted
that rival
the clay sculpture
             in lak ech
masterpieces of joy
that grace
the gallery
of her garden . . .

             Mangiamo! Virginia
                   . . . truth is, you are out
                   to sabotage my diet
                   but my taste buds drool
                   in shame:
                         May I have a
                         second helping?

Tonantzin Morena

a la memoria de mi madre
a mis hermanas de sangre
y de raza

en la casa de mi madre
no se perdía nada:
   when the milk went sour
   she made us cornbread
     . . . en el chiquigüite grande
     apenas cabía
     el pan de maíz. . .

the peach trees
cuajados de fruta
y nos hacía conserva
   . . . trabajo pa todo el día
   bastante comida . . .
     always plenty to do
     plenty to eat
bajo el techo AmorMaterno

mi madre morena
con su hechura de diosa
dominando el espacio
   corazón abierto
   mente alerta
   manos a la obra
haciendo maravillas de manta:

   ¡ay mami, queremos ir al mitote
   de la onda proletaria!

. . . and she would spend
the night sewing
       Adelita blouses

51

adding peasant ruffles
de retazos
to lengthen
our mini-skirts . . .

Mamá Tonantzin
always harnessing problems
always ready
with a sharp eye
for possibilities:
Oyes, hija, ven acá!!!
a dónde vas
con esos costales . . . ?

La Malinche A Cortez y Vice Versa

(o sea, "El Amor No Perdona, Ni Siquiera Por Amor")

ELLA: Dame tu nombre, mi amo y señor,
       para que me adorne.

              Cómo quisiera
grabarlo aquí, junto con el mío
en la arena. Es que soy tuya
y quiero que lo sepa
todo el mundo.

EL: Todo el mundo
     ya lo sabe
     mi querida Marina.

              No necesitas
adornos superfluos.
Yo te quiero y eso basta.

    Y entre paréntesis El se dijo:

Además, hrrrmmmppp!!! es indigno
que un hombre blanco
de mi noble estatura

              se enlace

con una sencilla esclava, hrrrmmmppp!
Es cierto,
        es una hembra

        olé! a todo dar . . .

pero no. Esta chatita patarajá
ya se está haciendo

demasiadas ilusiones, hrrrmmmppp!!!

ELLA: Sí, amo y señor mío, tienes razón.
Ya lo sé que me quieres
y perdona mi necedad.

                        Es que nosotras
las mujeres
siempre soñamos con imposibles . . .

Y entre paréntesis ELLA se dijo:

Hunh- y para eso te di
mi sangre y mi pueblo!
Sí, ya lo veo, gringo desabrido,
tanto así me quieres
que me casarás
con tu subordinado Don Juan,
sin más ni más
como si fuera yo
un kilo de carne
—pos ni que fueras mi padre
pa' venderme a tu antojo
güero infeliz. . . .

                             !!!

Etcétera

            etcétera.

Mona Lisa: Marguerite

at twenty   veinte abriles
she wants no part   y no es partidaria
of the
new
morality
modern Mona Lisa   Mona Lisa moderna
today's young flower   florecita de hoy
greenhouse grown
exquisite-nurtured
with yesterday's
values

I like the way
her Capricorn head
sits squarely
—bien escuadra—
upon her
soft-firm
shoulders

Chicanita Flor del Campo

Que sea yo linda-linda
    para ti
    pero no con adornos falsos
       eyes tinted
       lips painted
       hair waved and perfumed

sino por estas
    tortillas de cariño
    que amaso
       día tras día . . .

"San Antonio Rose" Was Chicana

demure by day
under a canopy
of shy-blue lids

tus ojos
        acerinas
        de noche
light their dazzling fires
to the melody
   of your voice
   guitarra chicana

the night
put to shame
quietly gathers
its stars

De Compras

Mis ojos
   empty saucers of yearning
   go window-shopping

     :los trajes
     más lindos
       always behind glass
       como sueños azules

       ethereal dreams
       —never a reality
       within my hands.

Tengo ganas
de vestirme
con lujo de seda

. . . acaso es pecado
alzar los ojos?

In the House of Love
or: "The Daily Soap Opera"

Death lurks
in the house of love:
I can smell
the acrid smoke
        of a pistol
        recently fired.

Caustic questions.
Mumbled answers.

My illusions
run for safety
like hysterical women
               helter-skelter
into the fraternity of corners:

   —Ya pasó: El Verbo Se Hizo Carne
   y tú, ni cuenta te diste.

   —The Word. ¿El Verbo? Oh I like
   The Noun. The working noun . . .
   so useful to poets.

   —Now me, I watch *Biografías*. Biografías
   Beatíficas Amo-Rosas . . .

   —Qué chistosa. No problems, huh?
   ¿Es que tienes la vida comprada?

   —Sí. Sólo que se la pasa
       e m p e ñ a d a . . .

—What! No MasterCharge? Hummmmmmmmh.
And I thought you had it made!
All the same, you were born
   with original sin . . .

—Y tú también. No lo niegues . . .
te dejaste llevar. Muy dueña
de tu vida.
        Tú, nuestra voz.
        Y ahora . . .
por tu estúpida culpa
vamos todas al paredón.

—Pues yo no. De aquí yo no
me muevo. Yo soy *La Dame Immobile.*

——¡Uuuyyy qué va! No se asusten
pero ya cayó mi corazón.
      Sin delito le tronaron.
      No hubo juicio.
            Ni razón.

Un relajito de primera . . .

. . . Let the passionflower
bloom again
        pregnant with hope
and along will come
incredible obstacle
      after obstacle
           like the curse
           of the mummy
so now the writer
   plumb out of obstacles
turns to the credible
   and only succeeds
      in boring the audience.
The audience complains.

Next day
Boss phones:

        ¡¡¿¿De Hoyos??!!
        Want to see you
        in my office.
                 Pronto!!!

Writer sputters:

        But-but this is what
        the women want . . .
        they want the whole
        take-me-out-of-the-kitchen
        fantasy bit.

Boss agrees:

        They want fantasy?
        Fine! Let 'em eat soap.
        Just make it edible.
        For your sake . . .
             and for my pocket.
        You know the formula . . .

—Yessir. Absolutely. Rightaway sir.

Writer exits. Dashes to desk:

                 Quick!
Where's my *Writer's Gospel?* . . . where's
my *Formula For Soap* . . . ahhhhhhhhhh!
  Ten Essentials: *How to Produce Soap.*
  How To Seduce An Audience.
    Audience = The Magic Word . . .
 . . . the word . . . the word eludes me. . . . . .

Writer becomes visibly distracted.
    (Remembers the time
    she missed a line.)

                                    Her frustration

turns to paranoia:
                              Looks up and sees
                              a million inimical faces
                              peering
                              into boob-tube.

Her stomach somersaults as the stage begins
to shake. She allows herself one long
close-up scream before she turns and runs.
Last
        thing
                heard
                        was
she joined the *Arts n Science* neo-KKK
                              (Kulture Kritters Klan)
                              where she hopes
                              to find
an acceptable euthanasia

. . . so she can put
        hero-heroine-writer
                out of (in)termina(b)l(e) misery.

A Man Can Grow Old

(y también nosotras las mujeres nos cansamos)

Saciada ya de luz
quise escurrirme
entre la noche
    noche de luto
              espesa
    sin estrellas ni luna
porque necesitaba
un descanso largo
    como de tumba.
    Y cerré la puerta.

Definitivamente.

. . . entonces por dónde judas
entran estos múltiples recuerdos
    recuerdos temporales
    como gusanos insistentes
infiltrándose en mi cuerpo
que a poro abierto grita:
    por Dios! que ni en la muerte
      existe
        paz . . . ?

Ancient History

(with apologies to Leo)

in the lion's den
    only
    the
    lion
    roars
?????????????????

Poema (Tema para Canción) de Despecho

era poca cosa
lo que entonces te pedía
—a lo más necesitaba
        un abrazo
        amigohermán

pero mi alma soñadora
era la que te imploraba
y tú no lo comprendiste
        porque no
        sabes amar

ya la barca de ilusiones
llega sobre la marea
de su carga de sortijas
        mira . . .
        qué te compraré?

que tú luzcas como prenda
y recuerdes por doquiera:
el amor que me negaste
        media vuelta
        y lo olvidé.

Realidades Macabras a la Rulfo

Cállate pero ya
   ya no me hables
      —el hombre le decía.
Al cabo cuando me hablas
   no te escucho. Hablas
      y hablas y nada dices
        . . . para qué hablas?

No platiques.   No platiques
con la gente.
        Pensarán
        que buscas algo
        para desaburrirte
. . . como que
      no estás conforme . . .

y eso
no me cuadra.

No te rías.
     Solo tú
     te ríes
     a boca abierta.
Yo no veo a nadie
reírse como tú te ríes.

Uuuuuujale. Otra vez
vas a llorar.

     No llores.

No te das cuenta
que te ves muy fea

—pareces gata enferma
cuando lloras.

Hasta que de tanto oír
no hables
    no platiques
        no te rías
            no llores
—sin llanto ya
sin voz
    sin boca-vocabulario
    sin belleza propia
        de mujer inviolable—
            un día
            la mujer
            amaneció
            muda.

"Si Amas, Perdona
Si No Amas, Olvida . . ."

                    that man
        that vulgar luckless man
            who spoke
            with a savage tongue
                (aunque el pueblo
                    estaba de fiesta)

        who spat
        those unkind words
        when you approached him

                    no, no sé si es chicano
                    —podría ser
                            cualquier hombre—
                    pero ese hombre
                    que tú me pintas
                        así, tan distinto
                        no lo conozco

        . . . still, he could be
            someone's brother
                        he must be
                        somebody's father . . .

        but supposing he were your own
        hermano carnal
        sólo que, por falta de luz
        aquel día
                    en su espacio cúbico
                    en su mundo insólito
            no te reconoció

or again, what if some day
you should happen
to come upon him
non-communicative
                    reduced
to the last corner of his
own private hell
        —toothless eyeless voiceless
                    casi deshecho
                    barely a shadow
                    on the wall—

and what if he sees you
as the last
frontier of his hope

        but you've come looking
                for roses, as in poetry
                for perfection, as in love

and he is only a derelict
devoid of all human dignity

so he has nothing
        nothing to give you
        beyond a blasphemous
                        inhuman
                        snarl.

ARTE
PUBLICO
PRESS